British Recipes

A Recipe Book For Cupcakes, Biscuits and Homemade Sweets

A selection of
British favourites

Diana Baker

Copyright © 2014 - 2016 Diana Baker

Copyright ©2014 - 2016 Editorial Imagen.
Córdoba, Argentina

Editorialimagen.com
All rights reserved.

Corrected and Revised Edition, February 2016

All rights reserved. No part of this book may be reproduced by any means (including electronic, mechanical or otherwise, such as photocopying, recording or any storage or reproduction of information) without written permission of the author, except for brief portions quoted for review purposes.

All images in this book (cover and interior pictures) are used with permission of: Ajwflickr, Red Mixser, Eljay, Psd, Usagede, Afeitar, Momo1976, Slgckgc, The Culinary Geek, Stu Spivack, Jamie Anne, Per Pettersson, Poppet with a camera, The Pink Princess, IkeX, Azartaz, Megan Khines, Pauline Mak, CookingCinderella, Tawest64, Volantra, Janet Hudson, Mike Saechang, jeffreyw, karenandbrademerson, surlygirl, Dichohecho, Whologwhy, Vanessa Lollipop, Steve A Johnson, Rafel Miro

CATEGORY: Recipes

Printed in the United States of America

ISBN-13:9781539413431
ISBN-10: 1539413438

Contents

Introduction 1

Hints to Ensure Success 3

To Prove the Temperature of the Oven 5

Weights and Measures 7

Key Recipes 9

    Scones 11
    Rough Puff Pastry 12
    Short Crust Pastry 13

Recipes for Small Cakes 15

    Atholl Crescent Rock Cakes 17
    Australian Spiders 18
    Baking Powder Biscuits 19
    Brown Biscuits 20
    Cinnamon Biscuits 21
    Cornflour Afternoon Tea Biscuits 22
    Cornflour Biscuits 23
    Empire Biscuits 24
    Ginger Biscuits 25
    Honey Biscuits 26
    Oatmeal Biscuits 28
    Shrewsbury Biscuits 29
    Brandy Snaps 30
    Hot Breakfast Cakes 32
    Hot Cross Buns – without yeast 33
    Hot Cross Buns – with yeast 35
    Chocolate Squares 36
    Toll House Chocolate Cookies 38
    Chimneys 40

Coconut Puffs	41
Norwegian Doughnuts	42
Eccles Cakes	43
Cream Puffs	46
Eclairs	47
Egg Creams	49
Fairy Cakes	50
Ginger Nuts	51
Ground Rice Tartlets	52
Cornflake Macaroons	53
Meringues	54
Meringues – II	54
Coconut Meringues	55
American Muffins	56
Nut Cakes	58
Oatmeal Squares	59
Oat Cakes	60
Oat Flapjacks	61
Fruit Oatmeal Cookies	62
Fancy Orange Cakes	63
Fancy Orange Cakes	64
Parkin	65
Perkins	66
Sponge Perkins	68
Potato Cake	69
Drop Scones	70
Royal Navy Drop Scones	71
Griddle Scones	72
Griddle Cakes	73
Granny's Scones	74
Sweet Breakfast Scones	75
Liberty Scones	76

Danish Spirals 77

Sultana Slices 78

Date Squares 79

Nursery Tea Cakes 80

Vinegar Cakes 81

Walnut Dream Bars 82

Walnut Fingers 83

Sour Cream Waffles 84

Plain Waffles 85

Homemade Bread 87

Date Bread 89

Swedish Brown Bread 90

Caraway Seed Bread 92

Currant Loaf 93

Canadian Date and Nut Loaf 94

Honey Bread 95

Fruit Bread 96

Nut Bread 97

Nut and Raisin Bread 98

Peanut Bread 99

Walnut Loaf 100

Yeast Bread 101

Homemade Sweets and Candy 103

Tips for Making Sweets 105

Special Points for Boiling Sugar 106

Degrees of Heat for Making Syrup 107

Recipes for Homemade Sweets 109

Barley Sugar 111

Butterscotch 112

Butterscotch – II 113

    Candy 114

    Cream Candy 115

    Caramels 116

    Caramel Coating for Sweets 117

    Chocolate Creams 118

    Chocolate Nut Bars 119

    Coconut Ice 120

    Coconut Ice – II 122

    Snow Dates 123

    Frosted Fruits 124

    Caramel Sweets 125

    Fondant 126

    Fruit Balls 127

    Chocolate Fudge 128

    Brown Sugar Fudge 130

    Divinity Fudge 131

    Nut Fudge 132

    Tutti Frutti Fudge 133

    Marshmallows 134

    Nougat 135

    Peanut Bricks 136

    Peppermint Creams 137

    Peppermint Creams II 138

    Peppermints 139

    Candy Oats 140

    Toffee 141

    Turkish Delight 142

Icings 143

    American Icing 145

    Butter Icing 146

    Coffee Icing 147

Hard White Icing	148
Never-fail Icing	149
Never-fail Chocolate Frosting	150
Nut Filling and Icing	151
Sea-breeze Frosting	152

Fillings 153

Delicious Chocolate Filling	155
Filling for Leftover Egg Yolks	156
Lemon Cheese Filling	157
Synthetic Cream	158

More Books 161

Spanish Related Books 163

Introduction

Welcome to this recipe book for delicious cupcakes, biscuits, scones, waffles, homemade bread, icings, fillings and homemade sweets including many popular English favourites for the traditional afternoon tea when something good and sweet is a must.

In fact, any time of day is the right time for a biscuit especially if children are around! So it's a good idea to keep some in stock and homemade biscuits are better tasting!...have them ready for a snack, a bedtime treat, for the school lunch box or picnics and even for a surprise visitor.

And for the special occasion you can tempt anyone with a sumptuous homemade --sweet, no one will say no to.

You'll find the following recipes are really quick and easy to follow and prepare, using common and uncomplicated ingredients.

I'm sure you'll find many recipes will become long-time favourites in your home.

Let's begin with some helpful tips to ensure that nothing goes wrong.

Hints to Ensure Success

- Always read the recipe through carefully and understand it before starting. Then collect together and prepare all the ingredients to be used.

- Always sift the flour.

- Always stir in the same direction.

- Grease all cake tins except when making angel and sponge cakes.

- Never bang the oven door.

- Always work neatly; use as few utensils as possible, and clear up as the cooking proceeds.

- Never mix new flour with old.

- Never begrudge the time you spend on good mixing.

Cakes are often spoiled by over beating after the baking powder has been added; it is therefore advisable to add the baking powder, sifted with a small quantity of the flour, last.

One's usual experience is that if you take no care and make a hurried cake for the family, it is lighter than the cake made for the special occasion. The reason is probably because too much beating has been done after baking powder has been added, or that too much flour has been used.

To Prove the Temperature of the Oven

A simple and effective method of proving the heat of the oven when no thermometer is available:

Heat the oven for 10 minutes, then, put a piece of white paper in the centre of the oven. The temperature of the oven will be correct if the paper becomes brown in the time specified below:

Oven	Degrees	Paper
Very hot	446ºF–500ºF	½ minute
Hot	392ºF-428ºF	1 minute
Moderate	338ºF-374ºF	1 ½ minutes
Slow	320ºF	2 minutes

Electric and Gas equivalents

275°F = 140°C or Gas Mark 1
300°F = 150°C or Gas Mark 2
325°F = 165°C or Gas Mark 3
350°F = 180°C or Gas Mark 4
375°F = 190°C or Gas Mark 5
400°F = 200°C or Gas Mark 6
425°F = 220°C or Gas Mark 7
450°F = 230°C or Gas Mark 8

Weights and Measures

All containers used for measuring should be filled level, unless otherwise stated in the recipe, smoothing off any surplus with a knife.

When a cup is indicated, a cup holding ½ pint should be used.

1 Teaspoon equals 5 g or 60 drops

1 Dessertspoon equals 10 g or 2 teaspoons

1 Tablespoon equals 15 g or 3 teaspoons

1 wine glass equals 100 g or 4 tablespoons

1 cup equals ½ pint or ¼ litre or 16 tablespoons

1 lb. equals 16 ounces or 460 g

½ lb. equals 8 ounces or 230 g

1 ounce equals 28 ½ g

3 ½ cups flours are equivalent to .... 480 g or 1 lb.

2 cups oatmeal flour................................ 480 g or 1 lb

2 cups granulated sugar .... 400 g or 14 ozs

2 ½ cups icing sugar................................ 300 g or 11 ozs

2 1/4 cups brown sugar............................ 500 g or l lb.

1 cup seedless raisins .... 200 g or 7 ozs

1 cup currants etc. .... 200 g or 7 ozs

2 cups chopped nuts .... 240 g or ½ lb.

1 cup butter or lard .... 230 g or ½ lb.

Key Recipes

The following are basic recipes which allow you to use the variation preferred.

Scones

2 cups flour
A pinch of salt
4 teaspoons baking powder
4 tablespoons butter
1 egg
A little sugar (optional)
½ cup milk approximately

Sift together the flour, baking powder and salt. Rub in the butter.

Add beaten egg mixed with milk.

Roll out ½ inch thick.

Cut in circles and place on greased pan.

Bake in hot oven for 10 minutes.

Serve hot and well buttered, with cheese or jam in the middle.

Rough Puff Pastry

1½ cups flour
4 to 6 tablespoons lard and butter mixed
A pinch of salt
A few drops of lemon juice
A little ice water for mixing
A little baking powder (optional)

Sift the flour and salt into a bowl.

Put in the fat and cut it up into pieces the size of a half walnut.

Mix the lemon juice with a very little water and add to the pastry, mixing with a knife to a stiff dough.

Turn the pastry out onto a floured board, knead lightly to remove creases, roll out to an oblong strip about 14 inches long and 6 inches wide.

Mark into three; fold the bottom up to the middle and the top over it.

Give it one half turn and roll out again.

Repeat this three times.

Put it away to cool for as long as possible and use it for the same purposes as flaky pastry.

At first a very hot oven is required, reducing the heat towards the end of the cooking if necessary.

Short Crust Pastry

2 cups flour
¾ cup shortening
2 tablespoons sugar
2 teaspoons baking powder
A pinch of salt
2 tablespoons of very hot water

Rub the fat into the flour and baking powder then stir in the sugar and salt.

Add the water and when all is mixed, knead well with your hands.

Bake about 20 minutes in a hot oven.

(This does equally well for a meat pie by substituting more salt and a little pepper for the sugar).

Recipes for Small Cakes

Atholl Crescent Rock Cakes

3 tablespoons butter
2 cups flour
3 tablespoons sugar
1 egg
¼ teaspoon essence of lemon
¾ teaspoon baking powder
A little milk
Currants or fruit peel (optional)

Rub the butter into the flour.

Add the sugar and baking powder.

Mix in the well beaten egg and lemon essence and a little milk to gather the mixture nicely together, which should be fairly stiff.

Place upon a baking tin as roughly as possible and bake for about 15 minutes in a rather quick oven.

Currants or peel can be added if desired.

Australian Spiders

Makes about 2 dozen

½ lb chocolate
1 oz parrafin wax for cake making (sold at chemists)
½ cup mixed chopped nuts and sultanas
3 cups of cornflakes

Melt the chocolate and parrafin wax in a double saucepan.

When melted add the nuts, sultanas and cornflakes.

Take out the mixture in spoonfuls and put into well greased patty pans and press well together to make it adhere into little shapes like spiders.

Alternative mixture:

2 cups chocolate
1 oz parrafin wax

Melt in double saucepan and add:

½ cup chopped nuts
1 cup sultanas
3 cups oats

Baking Powder Biscuits

2 cups flour
4 teaspoons baking powder
2 tablespoons lard
¾ to 1 cup milk
1 teaspoon salt

Mix and sift dry ingredients.

Work in lard with finger tips and gradually add the milk.

Roll to ½ inch thick and cut with a biscuit cutter.

Brush over with milk and bake in a hot oven 12 to 15 minutes.

Brown Biscuits

2 cups brown flour (wholemeal)
1 cup white flour
¼ cup sugar
1 teaspoon salt
2 teaspoons baking powder
¾ cup milky water, approximately

Mix the dry ingredients well.

Now rub in 1 1/4 cups of butter.

Add the milky water.

Roll out very thin on well floured table.

Cut into shapes, place on cold baking sheet and bake in moderate oven until crisp, from 20 to 30 minutes.

Cinnamon Biscuits

2 tablespoons butter
4 tablespoons sugar
1 egg
8 heaped tablespoons flour
½ tablespoon cinnamon or ginger
1 teaspoon baking powder
A very little milk

Beat the butter and sugar to a cream.

Add the flour, baking powder and cinnamon and mix together.

Make into a stiff paste with egg and milk.

Knead a little and roll out thinly.

Cut into circles.

Sandwich the circles with raspberry jam and press the edges well together.

Bake in hot oven.

Cornflour Afternoon Tea Biscuits

¾ cup flour
¾ cup cornflour (cornstarch)
1 teaspoon baking powder
3 tablespoons butter (3 ozs)
3 tablespoon sugar
1 egg

Sift and mix dry ingredients and rub in the butter.

Then mix with the beaten egg.

Roll out and cut with biscuit cutter.

Bake in quick oven.

When cold, sandwich the biscuits with butter icing, flavoured with lemon juice.

Butter Icing:

2-3 ozs butter
1 cup approximately icing sugar
Lemon juice
A litle lemon rind (optional)
A pinch of salt

Cream the butter.

Add sifted sugar, salt and vanilla.

Beat together to a smooth paste.

Cornflour Biscuits

1 cup cornflour (cornstarch)
½ cup flour
1 egg and 1 yolk
½ cup sugar
½ cup butter
½ teaspoon baking powder
Vanilla essence
A pinch of salt

Sift and mix dry ingredients and rub in the butter.

Then mix with the beaten egg.

Roll out and cut with biscuit cutter.

Bake in moderate oven.

When cold, sandwich the biscuits with jam or caramel and cover the edges with coconut.

Empire Biscuits

4 tablespoons butter
½ cup sugar
1 egg
1 cup flour
½ teaspoon baking powder
1 teaspoon cream of tartar

Beat sugar and butter to a cream.

Add the egg and other ingredients.

Knead into a soft dough.

Roll out very thin.

Cut in circles.

Bake in a quick oven for 10 minutes.

Serve as sandwich with icing or jelly in between.

Ginger Biscuits

1 cup butter
4 cups flour
1 cup sugar
1 dessertspoon ground ginger
1 teaspoon ground cloves
1 cup golden syrup
1 heaped teaspoon bicarbonate of soda
1 tablespoon cold water

Rub butter into flour.

Add the spices and sugar then, the golden syrup, water and soda.

Roll out thin.

Cut into small circles and bake in a quick oven.

Honey Biscuits

This quantity will make about 20 biscuits.

5 tablespoons castor sugar
4 tablespoons butter (4 ozs)
1 egg yolk
1½ self-raising flour
1 teaspoon ground cinnamon
2 tablespoons honey

For coating:

2 dessertspoons castor sugar
¼ teaspoon ground cinnamon

Beat the sugar and butter to a cream.

Add the egg yolk and stir the mixture quickly for a minute.

Sift the flour and cinnamon and stir it gradually into the mixture, moistening it with the honey, warmed slightly to melt it.

Put the paste aside in a cool place until it becomes workable.

Then turn it onto a slightly floured board and divide it into small portions.

Form each portion into a smooth ball.

Coat them with castor sugar and cinnamon previously mixed together.

Place biscuits on a baking sheet, leaving a good space between each.

Bake in moderate oven about 15 minutes.

Cool them on a cake rack.

When cold, store in an air tight tin.

Oatmeal Biscuits

1½ cups oatmeal flour
1½ cups white flour
4 tablespoons butter
2 tablespoons sugar
1 teaspoon salt
1 teaspoon baking powder
1 egg
A little milk or water

Mix the flour and oatmeal together.

Rub in the butter.

Add salt, baking powder and sugar.

Beat the egg and add to it a little water or milk and mix with the other ingredients to a stiff dough.

Turn on to a floured board.

Roll till ¼ inch in thickness.

Prick well. Cut into circles or squares.

Place on a greased tin and bake in a moderate oven for 15 to 20 minutes.

If the egg is omitted a little more milk should be used.

Shrewsbury Biscuits

4 tablespoons butter
3 heaped tablespoons castor sugar
4 heaped tablespoons flour
1 egg

Beat butter into a cream.

Add the sugar then, the beaten egg and lastly the flour.

Allow it to stand in cool place and afterwards roll out on well floured board and cut into shapes.

Bake in moderate oven.

Brandy Snaps

4 tablespoons butter
½ cup castor sugar
½ cup flour
4 tablespoons golden syrup
¾ teaspoon ground ginger
A few drops vanilla essence

Put the butter, sugar and syrup into a saucepan and allow them to melt over the fire.

Sift the flour and mix it in gradually off the fire.

Add the ginger and vanilla.

Have ready one or two well greased tins.

Pour the mixture on to them in small lumps and then bake in a moderate oven.

When ready, remove the snaps with a palette knife, twist them round the handle of a wooden spoon and remove them when cold.

Time to bake is 10 minutes.

Fill with whipped cream just before serving.

If to be used as a sweet, a few drops of brandy in the cream prove a great improvement.

They are also delicious filled with whipped cream and prunes.

Hot Breakfast Cakes

1 tablespoons butter
2 cups flour
1 teaspoon bicarbonate of soda
2 teaspoons cream of tartar
1 teaspoon sugar
1 egg
1 small teaspoon salt
About 1 cup of milk

Rub the butter well into the flour.

Add the salt, sugar and cream of tartar perfectly free from lumps.

Add soda dissolved in a little milk.

Then add the whole egg without beating.

Add more milk and mix until it is a stiff batter.

Butter 2 dozen patty tins and put a large teaspoonful of the mixture into each one.

Bake in a quick oven for 10 minutes.

When cooked split open and butter well.

Serve hot.

Hot Cross Buns – without yeast

1 lb flour
1 teaspoon salt
1 teaspoon mixed spice
4 teaspoons baking powder
2 ozs lard
3 ozs sugar
3 ozs currants
2 ozs cut peel
1 beaten egg (put aside a spoonful for topping)
½ pint of water

Sift together the flour, salt, baking powder and spice in a bowl.

Rub in the lard and add the sugar, currants and peel.

Mix into soft dough with egg and water.

Divide into 12 portions and make into buns.

Place on greased baking sheet.

Make deep right-angled cuts across the tops of the buns with a knife and brush over with beaten egg.

Bake in hot oven for 15 minutes.

Hot Cross Buns – with yeast

1½ lbs flour
3 ozs lard
6 teaspoons sugar
1½ teaspoons salt
1½ ozs currants
1½ ozs sultanas
1 oz candied peel
1½ ozs yeast
A pinch of salt
¾ pint lukewarm milk and water

Rub the lard into the flour.

Add the salt, currants, sultanas, nutmeg and peel.

Make a hole in the middle of the flour, crumble in the yeast.

Add sugar and ½ pint of warm milk and water.

Leave tin in a warm place until the yeast begins to ferment.

Mix to a soft dough, adding remainder of milk.

Cover with a cloth and leave to rise for 45 minutes.

Shape dough into buns and lay them separated on a greased baking sheet.

Leave to rise for 10 minutes more.

Mark a cross on the tops with the back of a knife.

Brush with beaten egg.

Bake in quick oven 15 to 20 minutes.

Chocolate Squares

If left in a closed tin without turning out this cake will keep quite fresh for two weeks.

½ cup butter
1 cup sugar
2 eggs
1 1/3 cups flour
2 teaspoons baking powder
1 bar chocolate
¾ cup milk

Cream the butter and sugar. Add the well beaten egg yolks.

Melt the chocolate with the milk in a saucepan over fire.

Sift the flour with the baking powder and add to the first preparation alternately with the milk and chocolate.

Pour into a flat baking dish and bake in a moderate oven.

Cover with icing before turning out and cut into squares when needed.

Do not turn out to cool.

Toll House Chocolate Cookies

This recipe makes 100 cookies. You can also make just half the recipe.

1 cup butter or ½ cup butter and ½ cup margarine
¾ cup brown sugar
¾ cup moist sugar
2 eggs beaten whole
1 teaspoon bicarbonate of soda
1 teaspoon hot water
2¼ cups flour
1 teaspoon salt
1 teaspoon vanilla
1 cup chopped nuts
2 bars of sweet chocolate (7 ozs each)

Beat the butter into a cream.

Add the sugars and the 2 beaten eggs.

Dissolve the bicarbonate with the hot water and mix alternately with the mixture.

Add the flour and salt and lastly the nuts and chocolate which have been cut in pieces the size of a pea.

Flavour with the vanilla.

Drop by teaspoons on to a greased baking sheet.

Bake from 10 to 12 minutes in a moderate oven (374°F).

Tip:

Before starting your cookies, unwrap your bars of chocolate and put in a spot slightly warmer than room temperature (but do not melt). You will be surprised to see how easy it is to cut the bars into really small pieces.

Chimneys

This recipe makes about 15 little cakes.

6 tablespoons butter (6ozs)
½ cup sugar
1¼ cups flour
2 eggs and 1 yolk
2 spoonfuls baking powder
½ cup seedless raisins
Grated rind of ½ lemon

Beat the butter and sugar to a cream.

Add the egg yolks and whites separately, one at a time, beating constantly.

Then add the grated lemon rind.

Add slowly the sifted flour, mixed with the baking powder, and lastly the raisins.

Put into special tins (small, deep and round) but first put greaseproof paper at the sides.

Only fill to within ¾ of its capacity.

Cook in moderate oven for 25 minutes.

Coconut Puffs

3 eggs
1 cup castor sugar
1 tablespoon cornflour
2 cups grated coconut
1 teaspoon vanilla essence

Beat the whites of the eggs into a stiff froth.

Add the sugar slowly and the cornflour.

Place mixture in double saucepan and cook for 15 minutes, stirring constantly.

Then add the coconut and vanilla essence.

Drop the mixture into buttered tins and bake a delicate brown.

Norwegian Doughnuts

3 tablespoons butter
¾ cup sugar
2 eggs
3 cups flour
3 teaspoons baking powder
¾ cup milk
Salt and nutmeg to taste

Cream the butter and sugar.

Add unbeaten eggs and mix well.

Add dry ingredients alternately with milk.

Roll out thinly and cut into shapes with doughnut cutter.

Fry in deep lard until a golden brown.

Drain on paper.

Store in an airtight tin.

Eccles Cakes

Flaky, puff pastry although short crust pastry may be used if preferred - See below for recipe

For the filling:

1 tablespoon butter
4 tablespoons currants
2 tablespoons brown sugar
1 tablespoon finely cut candied peel
A little nutmeg
A little grated lemon rind

Put all into a bowl and stand near heat till quite dissolved. Mix well together.

Roll out the paste to about 1/4 inch thick. Cut into circles.

Brush the edges with beaten egg and put 1 or 2 teaspoons of the mixture in the centre.

Gather up the edges carefully. Turn the cakes on to a floured board and roll till the currants show through.

Sprinkle with sugar. Bake for about 10 minutes in hot oven.

Rough Puff Pastry:

1½ cups four
4 to 6 tablespoons lard and butter mixed
A pinch of salt
A few drops of lemon juice
A little ice water for mixing
A little baking powder (optional)

Sift the flour and salt into a bowl.

Put in the fat and cut it up into pieces the size of a half walnut.

Mix the lemon juice with a very little water and add to the pastry, mixing with a knife to a firm dough.

Turn the pastry out onto a floured board, knead lightly to remove creases, roll out to an oblong strip about 14 inches long and 6 inches wide.

Mark into three; fold the bottom up to the middle and the top over it.

Give it one half turn and roll out again.

Repeat this three times.

Put it away to cool for as long as possible and use it for the same purposes as flaky pastry.

At first a very hot oven is required, reducing the heat towards the end of the cooking if necessary.

Cream Puffs

1 cup water
2/3 cup butter
1½ cups flour
5 eggs

Put the water into a saucepan and when it boils add the butter and then the flour gradually.

Stir briskly for a moment until smooth.

When nearly cold stir in gradually the eggs, one at a time.

Drop on a greased tin and bake for about 30 minutes in a really hot oven.

When done they will be hollow and of a bright golden colour.

Cream for filling:

2 eggs or 4 yolks
2 cups milk
1/3 cup flour
1 cup sugar
A pinch of salt
A few drops of vanilla

Make into a thick custard in double saucepan and flavour with the vanilla.

When cold, cut bottom of cakes and fill with the mixture.

Eclairs

1 cup butter
2 cups flour
5 eggs
1 cup water
Cream for fillings – see below for recipe

Put the water and butter into a saucepan and bring to the boil.

Then add the flour, beating quickly with a wooden spoon.

Continue cooking for a few minutes over a slow fire.

Remove from fire, and add the eggs one by one, beating constantly until the mixture is smooth.

Leave it for a few minutes.

Then put by spoonfuls on to a buttered and floured baking sheet and cook for some 20 minutes in a moderate oven.

Fill with whipped cream or a chocolate cream. Dust over with icing sugar.

Chocolate cream filling for eclairs:

1 tablespoon flour
4 tablespoons sugar
2 eggs
2 cups milk
3 tablespoons chocolate, approximately
Essence of vanilla to taste

Put the flour in a bowl together with the sugar, eggs and vanilla.

Add the milk and the grated chocolate.

Put into a little saucepan to cook over slow fire stirring continually until it thickens.

The mixture must not boil.

Egg Creams

1 whole egg
1 yolk
1 tablespoon flour
4 tablespoons sugar
1¾ cups milk
½ stick vanilla or essence

Put the flour in a bowl together with the sugar, eggs and vanilla.

Add the milk.

Put into a little saucepan to cook over slow fire stirring continually until it thickens.

The mixture must not boil.

Fairy Cakes

3 cups flour (including 2 tablespoons cornflour)
1 cup butter
2 cups sugar
1 cup milk
5 eggs

Beat the butter, sugar and egg yolks until frothy.

Add the milk and flour alternately and lastly the whipped whites.

Bake in small tins, in a hot oven for about 15 to 20 minutes.

Ginger Nuts

2 cups flour
4 tablespoons butter (4 ozs)
4 tablespoons sugar (4 ozs)
1 tablespoon ground ginger
3 tablespoons golden syrup
½ teaspoon bicarbonate of soda

Cream together the butter and sugar.

Add syrup and the soda dissolved in a little cold water.

Add dry ingredients and mix into a stiff dough.

Pull off pieces the size of a nut and place on baking sheet with plenty of room to spread.

Bake in quick oven.

Ground Rice Tartlets

½ cup butter
½ cup sugar
1 cup of ground rice
¼ teaspoon baking powder
1 egg

Beat the butter, sugar and egg together then add the ground rice and baking powder.

Put layers of short pastry in small tart tins over which put a very little strawberry jam.

Then add the above mixture.

Cut little strips of pastry and form a cross over the tartlets.

Bake in a moderate oven.

Cornflake Macaroons

This recipe makes about 18 macaroons

2 egg whites
1 cup sugar
2 cups cornflakes
½ cup chopped nuts
1 cup ground coconut
½ teaspoon vanilla extract

Beat the egg whites until they are stiff enough to hold their shape.

Fold in sugar carefully.

Then add the cornflakes, nuts, coconut and lastly the vanilla.

Drop on well greased baking sheets.

Bake in moderate oven 15 or 20 minutes.

Meringues

6 egg whites
1 cup castor sugar
2 tablespoons lemon juice

Beat the egg whites until very stiff then add the sugar and the lemon juice.

Place in spoonfuls on a buttered pan and bake in slow oven.

Meringues – II

3 egg whites
1 cup castor sugar
A pinch of cream of tartar

Beat the egg whites until very stiff. Add the sugar and mix lightly with a wooden spoon.

Line a baking sheet with greaseproof and floured paper. Put the mixture by spoonfuls on to this.

Cook in oven at low temperature for about 40 minutes or until it will come away easily from the paper.

Remove from the oven and carefully turn each one over.

Place them again in the oven for a few minutes to dry with the oven door partly open.

Coconut Meringues

The whites of 6 eggs
12 tablespoons sugar
4 tablespoons coconut

Beat the whites of the eggs until stiff.

Add the sugar, coconut and stir with a wooden spoon.

Place in spoonfuls on a buttered pan and bake in a moderate oven for about 30 minutes.

American Muffins

This recipe makes 12 muffins.

2 cups flour
1 cup milk
½ cup sultanas
½ teaspoon salt
2 teaspoons baking powder
2 eggs
1 tablespoon sugar
4 tablespoons butter and lard mixed

Mix the dry ingredients and then add the eggs to the milk and mix with the flour, etc.

Add the melted butter and lard, and lastly the sultanas.

Cut in large circles.

Put on greased baking sheet.

Bake in hot oven for 25 minutes.

Serve hot.

Nut Cakes

½ cup butter
1 cup sugar
½ cup milk
2 cups flour
3 teaspoons baking powder
1 tablespoon vanilla essence
2 egg whites
¾ cup nuts, shelled

Cream the butter and gradually add the sugar.

Add the milk alternately with the baking powder and the flour sifted together.

Add the vanilla, the whites of the eggs beaten stiff, and the small bits of nuts.

Bake in buttered individual baking tins for about 20 minutes.

Oatmeal Squares

2 cups rolled oats
150 g raisins (optional)
4 tablespoons butter
2 tablespoons golden syrup
A pinch of salt

Place the oats in a bowl and rub the butter in well with finger tips.

Put the syrup into a saucepan and warm then mix into dry ingredients.

Have a greased flat baking sheet ready.

Turn the mixture into it, pressing nicely down, especially at the corners.

Bake in a slow oven for 30 minutes.

This mixture should be left to cool before cutting into squares.

Oat Cakes

½ cup rolled oats
¼ teaspoon salt
5 tablespoons warm water
½ tablespoon butter
¼ teaspoon bicarbonate of soda

Mix the oats with the salt.

Melt the butter in the warm water then add the bicarbonate of soda.

Pour the liquid into the oats and mix.

Divide into 4 small balls, roll out and cut in four.

Bake in a moderate oven for about 15 minutes.

Do not let them brown.

Oat Flapjacks

4 ozs butter
4 ozs brown sugar
5 ozs rolled oats

Melt together the butter and sugar.

Add the oats and mix all well together.

Press into a baking dish and bake in moderate oven for 15 minutes.

While still warm, cut into shapes with sharp knife.

Turn out when cold.

Fruit Oatmeal Cookies

Cream together:

½ cup butter or shortening
1 cup brown sugar
2 cups raw oatmeal
½ cup milk or fruit juice or cold coffee

Sift:

1 cup flour
2 teaspoons baking powder
½ teaspoon salt
1 teaspoon cinnamon
½ teaspoon each nutmeg, cloves and allspice

To this add:

1 cup raisins
½ cup chopped dates
¾ cup nuts
Grated rind of 1 orange

Add the flour and fruit mixtures to the first mixture.

Stir just enough to blend then drop by spoonfuls onto a buttered and floured baking sheet.

Bake in moderate oven for about 12 minutes.

Fancy Orange Cakes

The weight of 3 eggs in butter, sugar and flour
1 orange
1 teaspoon of baking powder
3 eggs
Icing sugar

Beat butter and sugar to a cream.

Add the eggs, then the flour, baking powder and the grated rind of the orange and if necessary, a little milk to make a stiff batter.

Pour into a flat baking sheet and bake in a fairly hot oven for 15 minutes.

When quite cold, spread with the icing sugar mixed with the juice of the orange.

Decorate with glacé cherries or walnuts.

When the icing is set, cut into squares.

Fancy Orange Cakes

The weight of 3 eggs in butter, sugar and flour
1 orange
1 teaspoon of baking powder
3 eggs
Icing sugar

Beat butter and sugar to a cream.

Add the eggs, then the flour, baking powder and the grated rind of the orange and if necessary, a little milk to make a stiff batter.

Pour into a flat baking sheet and bake in a fairly hot oven for 15 minutes.

When quite cold, spread with the icing sugar mixed with the juice of the orange.

Decorate with glacé cherries or walnuts.

When the icing is set, cut into squares.

Parkin

2 lbs fine oatmeal
3 ozs butter or lard
1½ lbs treacle or golden syrup
2 ozs brown sugar
½ oz ground ginger
Milk

Warm the treacle gradually until it is liquid.

Rub the lard or butter into the oatmeal.

Add the sugar, ginger and treacle.

Rinse out the saucepan which held the treacle, with beer or milk, and add gradually until the right consistency is obtained.

The mixture must be smooth, but must not drop too easily from the spoon.

Pour the mixture into greased tins and bake in a steady oven until the centre feels firm.

Cut into squares.

Perkins

1 cup flour
1 cup oatmeal
¼ teaspoon salt
1½ teaspoon baking soda
1 teaspoon cinnamon
1 teaspoon ground ginger
5 tablespoons sugar
2 tablespoons lard (2 ozs)
2 tablespoons treacle or syrup
A few almonds

Melt the lard and syrup in a small pan.

Add to dry ingredients and mix to a stiff dough.

Turn on to a floured board and form into flat circles like biscuits, about ¼ inch thick.

Put half an almond on each and place well apart on baking sheet. Bake for 20 minutes in moderate oven (356°F).

Cool slightly on the baking sheet before lifting on to a tray to cool.

Sponge Perkins

½ cup oatmeal and ½ cup flour or 1 cup flour and 4 ozs butter
½ cup brown sugar
2 tablespoons syrup
1 cup milk
1 egg
1 teaspoon ground ginger
1 teaspoon spice
1 teaspoon bicarbonate of soda

Mix all dry ingredients.

Melt the syrup and butter and add the warm milk, mixing well.

Add the dissolved bicarbonate of soda in it and add this to the mixture.

Lastly add the beaten egg.

Bake in a small square tin in a moderate oven for about 1 hour.

Cut in small squares while warm.

Potato Cake

1 lb potato flour
½ lb sugar
1 egg or 2 whites
½ lb butter beaten to a cream
10 drops lemon juice or 1 teaspoon grated rind of lemon

Mix the ingredients and beat them thoroughly for 10 minutes.

Then pour into a buttered cake tin and bake for 45 minutes in a moderate oven.

Drop Scones

1 cup flour
1 cup milk (slightly less)
1 egg
1 tablespoon sugar
1 teaspoon baking powder
A pinch of salt

Beat the egg.

Add flour and milk, beating till quite smooth.

Add sugar and lastly the baking powder.

Pour 1 tablespoon of the batter on to hot griddle.

Cook till it bubbles.

Turn with knife and cook on the other side.

Royal Navy Drop Scones

4 tablespoons melted butter
2 cups sifted flour
3 teaspoons baking powder
½ teaspoon salt
2 eggs
1¾ cups milk
1 spoonful sugar

Sift together the dry ingredients.

Add beaten eggs, milk and butter to the dry ingredients and mix well.

Drop by spoonfuls on slightly greased hot griddle.

When bubbles appear turn cakes and brown the other side.

Serve hot with butter.

If served with maple syrup, then omit the sugar in this recipe.

Griddle Scones

2 cups flour
1 small tablespoon butter
1 teaspoon syrup or sugar
2 small teaspoons cream of tartar
1 teaspoon bicarbonate of soda
¼ teaspoon salt
1 cup milk

Mix all the dry ingredients well together in the following order. The flour with the butter, syrup, salt and cream of tartar. Then mix to a soft dough with the milk in which the soda has been dissolved.

Cook on a floured griddle on top of stove.

Griddle Cakes

2½ cups flour
2 heaped tablespoons ground rice
1 tablespoon lard
2 heaped tablespoons sugar
2 teaspoons baking powder
1 teaspoon salt
½ teaspoon mixed spice
½ cup currants
1 cup cream and milk mixed

Mix well together the flour, rice, baking powder, spice, sugar and salt.

Then rub in the lard.

Add the cleaned currants, the milk and cream and mix to a fairly soft dough.

Roll out ¼ inch thick and prick all over with a fork.

Fry on a moderately hot griddle until browned on both sides.

Split and butter and serve hot.

Granny's Scones

3 heaped cups flour
1 teaspoon salt
4 ½ teaspoons baking powder
1 cup cream
1½ cups milk

Sift the flour and add the salt and baking powder. Mix well.

Make a hole in the middle of the flour.

Pour in the cream and milk.

Mix lightly but well.

Roll the mixture out but do not press.

Cut into shapes and place on cool baking sheet to cook in a quick oven for about 20 minutes.

When cooked, dip the top of each in creamy milk as soon as removed from oven.

Sweet Breakfast Scones

4 cups flour
4 teaspoons baking powder
½ teaspoon salt
½ cup butter
1 cup milk
2 eggs
4 tablespoons sugar
½ cup currants

Mix well the sifted flour, sugar, baking powder, currants and salt.

Rub in the butter.

Beat eggs lightly.

Add the milk to them.

Stir the liquid into the dry ingredients gradually.

Turn out on to pastry board and mix lightly until smooth.

Roll out about an inch thick and cut into the desired shapes and size.

Bake about 20 minutes in a quick oven.

Liberty Scones

2 cups flour
A pinch of salt
4 teaspoons baking powder
2 tablespoons butter
A little sugar (optional)
1 egg
½ cup milk, approximately

Sift together the flour, baking powder and salt.

Rub in the butter then add beaten egg mixed with milk.

Roll out ½ inch thick.

Cut in circles and place on greased pan.

Bake in hot oven for 10 minutes.

Serve hot and well buttered, with cheese or jam in the middle.

Danish Spirals

2 cups flour
¾ cup butter
½ cup castor sugar
1 cup almonds
1gg
¼ teaspoon carbonate of ammonium (from chemist's)
1 stick vanilla (using the inside only which has to be scraped with a knife)

Knead together the butter, sugar, sifted flour and ammonium with the egg, ground almonds and vanilla.

When the dough is well mixed, pass it through a mincing machine with a star shaped nozzle at the end (½ inch diametre).

Form spiral shapes from the dough and place on a baking sheet previously buttered.

Bake in moderate oven.

Sultana Slices

1¾ cups flour
2 teaspoons baking powder
4 tablespoons fat
1 dessertspoon sugar
3 tablespoons sultanas
A pinch of salt
Water to mix

Sift the flour, baking powder and salt.

Rub in the fat.

Mix with water to a stiff paste.

Divide into equal portions, one for **Date Squares** (see next recipe).

Roll pastry to a wide oblong shape, brush over with water, sprinkle with sultanas and then sugar.

Roll up like a roly-poly and cut into thick slices.

Lay these lightly on a greased baking sheet and bake in hot oven.

Date Squares

For the ingredients see the previous recipe.

Roll the remaining paste to oblong shape and cover half with dates, packing them closely.

Fold the other half over dates, and press down securely.

Roll over lightly with rolling pin.

Cut into squares and mark lines crosswise on each with fancy pastry cutter.

Brush with milk and bake in hot oven.

Nursery Tea Cakes

1 cup flour
½ teaspoon salt
1 teaspoon baking powder
2 eggs
1 cup sugar
4 tablespoons cold water

Separate 2 eggs, beat whites to a stiff froth, then, without washing the beater, beat yolks well.

Add gradually 2 cups sifted sugar and the cold water.

Add the flour, salt and baking powder which have been sifted.

Mix well.

Then add the beaten egg whites.

Grease a shallow baking pan and line with greased paper.

Spread batter out and bake in moderate oven for 10 minutes.

Cut the cake in diamond shaped pieces and ice them with icing sugar which has been melted with hot water or milk.

To make them more attractive one can add a few drops of colouring to half the icing, so that the two different colour cakes catch the eye.

Vinegar Cakes

No eggs are needed for this recipe.

2 tablespoons butter or lard
4 tablespoons sugar
1 cup flour
½ teaspoon baking powder
½ teaspoon bicarbonate of soda
¼ cup milk
A pinch of salt
1 tablespoon vinegar
2 tablespoon mixed peel
½ teaspoon mixed spice
½ cup raisins

Cream the butter and sugar together.

Add the flour and other ingredients and mix well.

Bake in a flat baking tin in moderate oven for about 20 minutes.

When cooked, cool and cut into pieces.

Walnut Dream Bars

¼ cup butter
1¼ cups flour
1¼ cups brown sugar
2 eggs
½ teaspoon baking powder
1 teaspoon vanilla
1½ cups coconut
1 cup chopped walnuts

1st Preparation:

Cut butter into 1 cup flour and ¼ cup brown sugar until mixture is of consistency of coarse meal.

Put this mixture into ungreased square cake tin and bake in moderate oven for 15 minutes.

2nd Preparation:

Beat eggs until light.

Then add the rest of the brown sugar gradually and beat well.

Fold in the remaining flour sifted with baking powder.

Add vanilla, coconut and walnuts and mix well.

Spread over the top of still warm mixture in pan and bake in moderate oven for 20 minutes or until crisp and brown.

While still warm, cut into squares.

Walnut Fingers

2 cups flour
2 tablespoons granulated sugar
½ cup butter (4 ozs)
1 teaspoon baking powder
4 tablespoons icing sugar
2 tablespoons chopped walnuts
1 egg
Apricot jam

Mix well all dry ingredients. Blend with the yolk of the egg using a little milk if necessary.

Roll out and line with this, a square buttered tin. Cover the pastry with apricot jam.

Slightly beat the white of egg with the icing sugar and spread all over pastry, covering the jam and sprinkle with the chopped nuts.

Cook in a moderate oven about 15 minutes. When ready, cut into fingers.

Sour Cream Waffles

This recipe requires an electric waffle iron.

Makes 5 waffles
2 tablespoons butter
1¾ cups flour
1 teaspoon baking powder
1 teaspoon bicarbonate of soda
½ teaspoon salt
2 eggs
1¼ cups sour cream

Sift and mix all dry ingredients.

Add well beaten egg yolks, cream and melted butter.

Fold in the stiffly beaten whites.

Heat waffle iron 8 minutes.

Pour ¾ cup batter into centre of plate and bake for 3 minutes.

Serve with honey or with strawberries and cream.

Plain Waffles

This recipe requires an electric waffle iron.

2 tablespoons butter
1¾ cups flour
1 teaspoon baking powder
1 teaspoon bicarbonate of soda
½ teaspoon salt
2 eggs
1 cup fresh milk
1 tablespoon sugar

Sift and mix all dry ingredients.

Add well beaten egg yolks, milk and melted butter.

Fold in the stiffly beaten whites.

Heat waffle iron 8 minutes.

Pour ¾ cup batter into centre of plate and bake for 3 minutes.

Serve with honey or with chocolate ice cream or whipped cream.

Homemade Bread

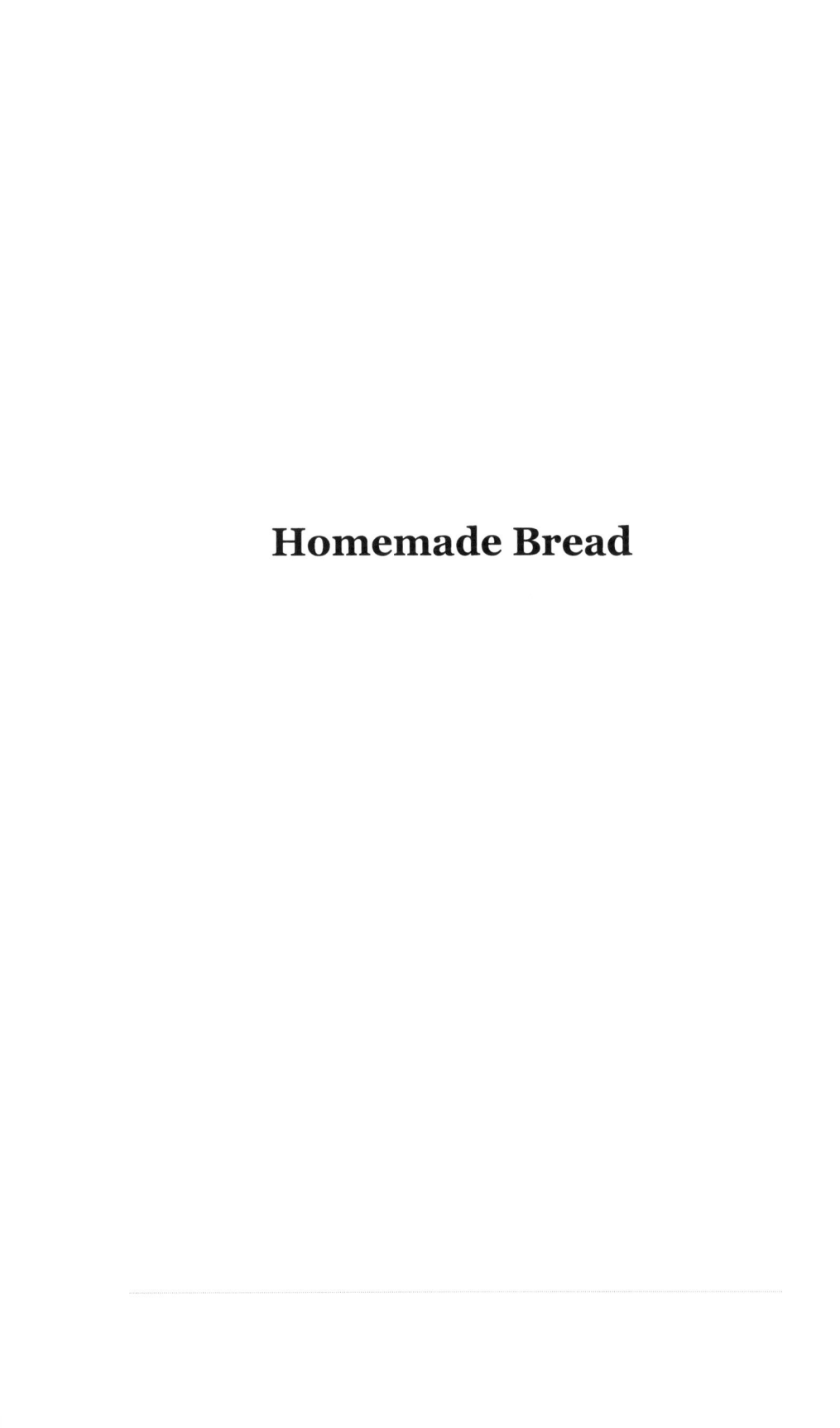

Date Bread

2 tablespoons butter
¾ cup sugar
1 egg
1¾ cups flour
1 teaspoon baking powder
1 teaspoon bicarbonate of soda
A pinch of salt
¾ cup dates
3 dessertspoons walnuts
¾ cup hot water

Cut dates in half.

Add the hot water and allow to cool.

Chop walnuts fairly fine and add to all other ingredients.

Then add the dates and water.

Bake in moderate oven for about 1 hour.

Swedish Brown Bread

2 tablespoons sugar
1 egg
1½ cups Graham flour
1½ cups white flour
4 teaspoons baking powder
1 teaspoon powdered caraway seeds
1½ cups milk and water
1 teaspoon salt

Mix together all the dry ingredients.

Add the egg, beaten in the milk and water.

Cook in a slow oven for 1 hour.

Alternative method:

3 cups Rye flour or half Rye and half wheat flour
2 teaspoons bicarbonate of soda
1 teaspoon baking powder

½ tablespoon liquorice
½ tablespoon anise
2 cups sour milk
1 cup golden syrup

Beat the milk and syrup.

Then add the dry ingredients.

Bake for about 1 hour in a slow oven.

When cooked, roll up in a towel to keep moist.

Caraway Seed Bread

5 ozs butter
½ cup sugar
3 cups flour
2 eggs
3 teaspoons baking powder
1 teaspoon caraway seeds
Milk

Mix all the ingredients together, adding lastly the well beaten eggs with sufficient milk to blend.

Make into a loaf shape.

Put in a greased tin and leave to rise about 15 to 20 minutes.

Brush it over with a beaten egg and cook in a moderate oven about 50 minutes.

Currant Loaf

½ cup sugar
4 cups flour
1 egg
1½ cups milk
4 teaspoons baking powder
1 teaspoon salt
1 cup currants

Beat the eggs with the milk.

Sift the flour, sugar, salt and baking powder.

Add the currants and then add the egg and milk mixture.

Make a fairly soft dough.

Turn into a buttered loaf pan and leave it to rise at the edge of the stove for about 20 minutes.

Then cook in a moderate oven for about 50 minutes.

Canadian Date and Nut Loaf

1 tablespoon creamed butter
1 cup brown sugar
1 egg
1½ cups flour
1 teaspoon bicarbonate of soda
1 cup chopped dates
½ cup chopped walnuts
Boiling water
Flavouring

Sprinkle baking soda over a cupful of chopped dates.

Fill up with the boiling water and set aside to cool.

Mix together in the following order: sugar, butter, flour, walnuts, unbeaten egg and flavouring.

Mix well and then add to this the date mixture.

Bake in well greased loaf pan in moderate oven for about 1 hour.

Honey Bread

½ cup butter
1¼ cups sugar
3 cups flour
1 teaspoon bicarbonate of soda
1¼ cups honey
½ cup water

Melt the butter, honey and sugar in the water over heat.

Then mix this into the flour to which has been added the bicarbonate of soda.

Put mixture into a loaf shaped tin slightly heated, with greaseproof paper at the bottom.

Bake in medium oven for 1 hour.

Fruit Bread

1 tablespoon butter or lard
½ cup sugar
1 egg
2 cups flour
4 teaspoons baking powder
1 teaspoon salt
¾ cup raisins or walnuts
1½ cups milk

Mix all ingredients, moisten with egg and milk.

Leave standing for about 80 minutes.

Bake till firm, in moderate oven about 20 minutes.

Nut Bread

This recipe stays fresh for several days.

2 cups flour
1 cup ground nuts
1 egg
1 teaspoon salt
3 teaspoons baking powder
1 cup milk

Sift together the flour, salt and baking powder.

Add the nuts and mix with the well beaten egg and milk.

Bake in a fairly hot oven for about 40 minutes.

Nut and Raisin Bread

½ cup sugar
3 cups flour
3 teaspoons baking powder
1 teaspoon cinnamon
1 beaten egg
1 cup milk
1 cup chopped nuts
1 cup raisins

Sift the dry ingredients together: the sugar, flour, baking powder and cinnamon.

Then add the beaten egg and the milk.

Add the nuts and raisins last.

Stir well and bake in moderate oven till well done, about 45 minutes.

Peanut Bread

4 tablespoons sugar
1 egg
2 cups flour
4 teaspoon baking powder
½ teaspoon salt
½ cup chopped peanuts
¾ cup milk

Mix dry ingredients.

Then add the egg and milk and stir slightly.

Bake in moderate oven for 35 minutes.

Walnut Loaf

¾ cup of castor sugar
1 egg
4 cups flour
4 teaspoons baking powder
1 teaspoon salt
2 cups milk
1 cup chopped walnuts

Mix all dry ingredients.

Beat the egg and add the milk.

Mix all together.

Put in a floured tin and let it stand in a warm place for 40 minutes.

Bake in moderate oven for 1 hour.

Yeast Bread

1 tablespoon sugar
3¼ lbs flour
3 tablespoons yeast
1 quart warm water mixed with 1 tablespoon salt

It is important to use the yeast as soon as possible after buying. Cover the yeast with a spoonful of sugar and leave for about 10 minutes. Then mix the yeast with warm water and salt.

Stir to a smooth paste, then make a hole in the centre and pour in the flour. Stir with a wooden spoon until well mixed.

Turn out onto a board or table and knead.

Then put back into a basin. Cover with a cloth and set to rise in a warm temperature, but not in the direct sun or a draught, for 2 hours.

Then put into floured tins and bake in a moderate oven.

To test if cooked, turn out one loaf and knock on the bottom. It should have a hollow sound.

It is best to turn off the gas but leave the loaves in the warm oven until quite cold with the oven door a little open.

Do not cut until the next day.

Homemade Sweets and Candy

Tips for Making Sweets

There may be a mistaken idea that sweet making cannot be attempted at home without a lot of expensive equipment.

A large sum of money can be spent easily on the fascinating little gadgets which one can buy especially for it, but it will be found, in most instances, that these can be substituted by the ordinary kitchen utensils and just a sugar boiler's thermometre. The latter is a real necessity for the boiling of syrups.

Some points need special consideration in the making of sugar syrups, which are the foundation of most cooked sweets.

Too much stress cannot be laid on their importance. They definitely must be observed if satisfactory results are to be obtained.

Special Points for Boiling Sugar

1. Use good quality sugar and measure it and the other ingredients accurately.

2. Dissolve the sugar entirely over gentle heat before the syrup boils.

3. Do not stir the syrup at all, unless directed to do so in the recipe.

4. To prevent the syrup hardening, brush round the pan with a brush previously dipped in hot water.

5. Do not shake the pan, or the syrup will crystallize.

Degrees of Heat for Making Syrup

Use granulated sugar unless otherwise specified.

Soft ball degree...................236ºF to 242ºF
Hard ball degree..................243ºF
Very hard ball degree.........248ºF
Soft crack degree................290ºF
Hard crack degree...............310ºF

Recipes for Homemade Sweets

Barley Sugar

6 cups sugar
1 cup water
½ teaspoon cream of tartar
Juice of 1 lemon

Put sugar, water and cream of tartar into a saucepan.

Stir until dissolved over low heat, after which boil quickly and add lemon juice.

Drop a little in cold water, and when it hardens it is done.

Pour on to a buttered slab and when slightly cool, cut into strips with scissors and twist.

When cold, put into air-tight tins.

Butterscotch

3½ ozs butter (½ cup)
1 cup sugar
2 dessertspoons vinegar
2 dessertspoons hot water
1 tablespoon golden syrup
A pinch of salt
Vanilla if desired

Melt the butter.

Add the rest of the ingredients and boil for approximately 10 minutes or until the syrup forms a hard ball when tested in cold water.

Pour into a shallow greased tin and when cold break into squares and fold in greaseproof paper.

Butterscotch – II

6 ozs butter
1 lb castor sugar
¼ lb golden syrup
Juice of ½ a lemon

Place all ingredients together in pan.

Bring to the boil, and then boil steadily for about 8 to 10 minutes.

Test a little in cold water.

When brittle it is done.

No need to stir, although an occasional stir is good.

Pour on to greased baking tin and before it is cold sear into squares with a knife and then it is easy to break.

Candy

2 cups sugar
2 tablespoons malt vinegar
1 teaspoon lemon extract
1 teaspoon cream of tartar

Moisten the sugar with a spoonful of water.

Boil with vinegar and cream of tartar without stirring until brittle when tested in water.

Add flavouring and turn out quickly on to buttered dish.

When cool enough to handle, pull until white and cut into pieces.

Cream Candy

1 ¾ cups sugar
1 cup cream
½ cup butter
¼ teaspoon cream of tartar
1 teaspoon of rum

Place sugar with cream of tartar in a saucepan.

Add the cream and boil for a few minutes, stirring with a wooden spoon.

Add the butter and allow to boil until very thick and a light brown colour, stirring constantly.

Add the rum.

Turn out on to a buttered plate.

Caramels

2 cups sugar
½ cup cold water
2 tablespoons butter
½ teaspoon cream of tartar
1 teaspoon vanilla

Put all the ingredients into a saucepan and boil until when tested in cold water it forms a ball.

Pour onto buttered plate to cool.

Caramel Coating for Sweets

1 cup white sugar
½ cup water
¼ teaspoon bicarbonate of soda
Vanilla essence

Mix all together and boil until it begins to solidify (300°F).

Chocolate Creams

½ lb sweet chocolate
5 tablespoons butter
4 egg yolks

Melt chocolate in a double boiler.

Put the butter into a bowl and beat until creamy.

Add the egg yolks one by one and lastly the cooled chocolate.

Let the mixture stand overnight in refrigerator.

Make into little balls, rolled into grated chocolate.

Chocolate Nut Bars

½ lb sweet chocolate
1¾ chopped raisins
¾ cup chopped pistachio nuts
A pinch of salt

Melt the chocolate in the top of a double boiler until smooth and almost cool.

Add salt, raisins and nuts.

Mix well.

Spread in a shallow buttered tin ¼ inch thick.

When set cut into short bars.

Coconut Ice

2½ cups castor sugar
1 cup water
2 cups coconut
Colouring

Boil the sugar and water together for 5 minutes then stir in the coconut and boil again for 10 minutes.

Spread half on white paper, colour the other half with a few drops of food colouring and spread on top of the white.

Remove from paper before quite cold and cut into squares.

Coconut Ice – II

1 coconut
½ lb sugar
2 tablespoons milk
Colouring

Grate 1 lb of the coconut. (Save the milk).

Put the sugar into a saucepan with the milk and when dissolved, add the grated coconut, taking care it does not burn.

Boil for 10 minutes.

Turn out onto a buttered slab.

Make into cakes and when nearly set, cut into blocks.

Use colouring for half of them.

Snow Dates

1 lb dates
½ lb nuts
Icing sugar

Take out the stones and refill the dates with a nut.

Roll them in granulated sugar.

Frosted Fruits

Dates or prunes
Sweet almonds
Icing sugar
Egg white
Walnuts
Marzipan
Lemon Juice
A few drops of colouring

Remove the stones from some dates or prunes.

Refill with a mixture made of sweet ground almonds mixed with icing sugar and the white of an egg.

Roll in castor sugar.

A variation:

Walnuts also make a nice sweet with the marzipan icing between the two halves of the nut.

These may be decorated with icing sugar mixed with lemon juice and a few drops of colouring.

Caramel Sweets

12 cups of milk
7 cups sugar
1 stick vanilla

Put the milk, sugar and vanilla in a saucepan over moderate fire, stir occasionally with a wooden spoon and let boil slowly.

When it begins to thicken a little stir constantly until it becomes difficult to continue.

Then remove from fire, continue stirring a little longer.

Then turn onto a buttered marble slab.

Leave to cool slightly.

Cut up into pieces with a buttered knife.

Fondant

Many delicious sweets may be made with this easily made fondant.

2 ½ cups icing sugar
1 teaspoon vanilla
½ cup sweetened condensed milk

Mix all together until smooth and creamy.

Any flavouring may be introduced such as oil of peppermint, almond or chocolate.

And it can also be tinted any colour.

Fruit Balls

1 cup prunes
1 cup seedless raisins
1 cup dates
1 cup nuts
1 cup figs
½ tablespoon cinnamon
A pinch of salt

Wash the prunes well and remove the stones from these and the dates.

Pound all and blend well together.

Make into small balls.

Roll each ball in castor sugar.

Chocolate Fudge

¾ cup of butter
6 bars chocolate (½ lb)
1 cup milk
2 cups sugar
1 cup chopped nuts

Boil over quick fire for 15 minutes.

Add the nuts.

Remove from fire and beat until the mixture thickens.

Turn out onto buttered plates.

Cut into squares.

Brown Sugar Fudge

3 cups brown sugar
¾ cups milk
Butter, the size of an egg

Put all in a heavy frying pan and cook rapidly, stirring continually.

It cooks in a few minutes.

When the froth begins to disappear test a little in cold water and it should form a soft ball.

Remove from fire and stir till it begins to solidify.

Turn onto a slightly buttered slab and when nearly cold, cut into squares.

Try any of the following variations:

- The juice of ½ a lemon or a little vinegar con be added when the milk has been stirred in.

- 2 bars of chocolate.

- 1 tablespoon honey or treacle – this makes a smooth fudge.

- 1 cup ground biscuits stirred in when it commences to solidify – this makes the sweet spongy.

Divinity Fudge

2 cups sugar
½ cup water
½ cup golden syrup
2 egg whites
1 teaspoon vanilla essence
1 heaped cup chopped nuts

Boil the sugar, water and syrup until it forms soft balls when dropped into cold water.

Beat the whites stiff and pour half the mixture on to them and beat well.

Cook the rest of the mixture until brittle and add to the first preparation.

Add vanilla and nuts.

Pour onto buttered flat dish and leave to set before cutting into squares.

Nut Fudge

2 cups brown sugar
½ cup cream
1 tablespoon butter
1 teaspoon vanilla essence
A pinch of cream of tartar
Chopped nuts

Put the sugar, cream, butter and cream of tartar into a saucepan and boil, stirring as little as possible, until the mixture forms a soft ball when a drop is tested in cold water.

Remove from the heat.

Add the nuts and vanilla.

Beat until it thickens.

Then pour into a buttered tin and when cold cut into squares.

Wrap each square in wax paper for packing.

Tutti Frutti Fudge

3 cups sugar
1 cup milk
Butter the size of an egg
½ cup fruit jelly – apple, plum etc. or use jam passed through a wire strainer

Cook rapidly in a frying pan, stirring well all the time.

Test frequently until it hardens in cold water, then remove from fire and stir vigorously till very nearly solid.

Pour on buttered marble slab or buttered plate.

Cut into pieces before it hardens.

Marshmallows

4 cups sugar
2½ cups water
4 tablespoons powdered gelatine
A pinch of salt
20 drops vanilla

Soak the gelatine for about 10 minutes in 1 cup cold water.

Put the sugar with the remaining water in a saucepan and let boil until a fine thread forms from the spoon.

Add the soaked gelatine and let stand until partly cooled.

Add the vanilla and salt. Beat with whisk until mixture becomes white and thick. (Chopped candied fruit and nuts may be added during the last minute beating).

Pour into a flat shallow dish that has been thickly dusted with icing sugar.

Nougat

1 cup sugar
½ cup water
3 tablespoons golden syrup
2 egg whites
½ cup strained honey
2 cups toasted shredded almonds
½ cup blanched pistachio nuts
1 teaspoon vanilla
Nougat wafers (optional)

Mix sugar, water and 1½ tablespoons of the syrup. Bring to boiling point, stirring until sugar is dissolved.

Then continue cooking to hard ball state.

When syrup is almost ready, beat egg whites until stiff but not dry.

Then add syrup slowly, beating constantly.

Add nuts.

Place over hot water and cook until mixture dries, stirring constantly. If a little taken out on a spoon holds its shape when cold and is not sticky to touch, the candy is ready.

Add vanilla.

Pour into pan lined with nougat wafers, although these may be omitted if desired. Cover with the pan or a board and press with heavy weight for at least 12 hours.

Remove block of candy and cut in squares. Wrap in waxed paper.

Turn candy into pan and when firm cut in squares.

Peanut Bricks

3 cups roasted and peeled peanuts
5 cups sugar

Put sugar in pan over a slow heat.

It will lump and then gradually melt.

When it is a pale coffee colour, throw in the peanuts and pour quickly on to a greased slab.

Break into pieces when cold.

Peppermint Creams

1 lb of icing sugar
1 tablespoon cream
20 drops oil of peppermint

Mix well, roll out and cut into rounds.

Leave to dry.

Then bottle.

Peppermint Creams II

This recipe uses a boiling method.

2 cups sugar
1 cup water
A pinch of cream of tartar

Put sugar and water into a saucepan and stir on fire till sugar is dissolved.

Stop stirring,

When it boils sprinkle the cream of tartar on and do not stir.

Boil until it forms a soft ball in cold water.

Take off fire and leave for 2 minutes then pour into a wet soup plate.

When cool, stir with a spoon till all hard and white, then work with the hands till free of lumps.

Put two or three drops of peppermint essence on your hands.

Work the whole piece well.

Roll out and cut with a cutter.

Leave to dry.

Peppermints

2 cups icing sugar
1 dessertspoon glucose or golden syrup
1 tablespoon boiling water
8 to 10 drops oil of peppermint

Mix the syrup or glucose together with the boiling water and drops of peppermint.

Then add the sugar.

Blend well.

Form into flat round shapes.

Dust well with icing sugar.

Note:

Stiffly beaten whites of 2 eggs may be substituted for the glucose.

Candy Oats

1 cup brown sugar
1 cup butter
1 cup rolled oats

Mix well together and bake in moderate oven for 15 minutes.

Turn out when cold.

Cut into small pieces.

Toffee

½ cup butter
1 cup sugar
1 tablespoon golden syrup
2 tablespoons hot water
1 tablespoon vinegar

Boil all the ingredients together until a small drop is brittle when tested in a cup of cold water.

Turkish Delight

1 oz gelatine
½ small cup of water
Juice of 2 lemons
1 lb loaf sugar
Rose essence
Icing sugar

Dissolve the gelatine in the water. Add the juice of the lemons together with the sugar.

Let it melt slowly then boil up quickly for 5 minutes.

Then add some rose essence.

Divide the mixture into 2 greased tins and colour one pink.

After 24 hours cut into blocks and toss in icing sugar.

Icings

American Icing

3 cups granulated sugar
2 egg whites
1 small cup water

Put the sugar and water into a clean saucepan and allow the sugar to dissolve slowly.

Bring to the boil, and allow to boil 6 or 7 minutes according to the rate of boiling, timing it from the moment the sugar has dissolved, and the mixture begins to boil; do not stir.

Meanwhile, whisk the whites to a very stiff froth in a large bowl, and when the syrup is ready pour over the whites, whisking all the time.

Continue stirring until the icing cools and thickens sufficiently to coat the cake thickly, at the same time running over it smoothly - very little should run off the cake.

It should set very quickly at this point and care must be taken not to whisk too long or the icing will not run.

Any remains of this icing, may be used as a filling between sandwich cakes etc.

Chopped nuts, apricot jam or fruit juice may be mixed with it.

Butter Icing

1/3 cup butter
2 cups approximately icing sugar
1 teaspoon vanilla
1/8 teaspoon salt

Cream the butter. Add sifted sugar, salt and vanilla.

Variations:

- Use lemon juice instead of vanilla and grated rind of lemon.

- Use orange and sprinkle coconut.

- Add 2 squares of melted bitter chocolate.

- Use strong black coffee to flavor.

Coffee Icing

2 cups icing sugar
1 egg yolk
A little strong coffee

Beat egg yolk well, pour over the hot coffee and add sugar until the right consistency to spread.

Cut the cake into layers and fill with chopped dates or with prunes that have been previously soaked in brandy.

Hard White Icing

3 cups granulated sugar
1 cup milk
1 pinch bicarbonate soda
1 teaspoon vanilla essence
A little lemon juice

Boil until a soft ball forms when tested in cold water.

Then add vanilla and lemon juice and beat until stiff.

Never-fail Icing

This recipe is ready in 4 minutes.

1 cup moist sugar
2 egg whites
¼ teaspoon cream of tartar
3 tablespoons water
Flavouring to taste

Place all ingredients in a double boiler over boiling water and beat constantly with an egg whisk.

Beat until the mixture leaves a hole when the beater is removed.

After removing from the fire continue beating until it is stiff enough to spread.

Never-fail Chocolate Frosting

1 bar sweet chocolate (7 ozs.)
2 tablespoons butter
1 cup sifted icing sugar
¼ cup hot milk

Melt chocolate over hot water.

Add butter and icing sugar.

Add hot milk slowly.

Beat until smooth and satiny, spread on cake.

Nut Filling and Icing

5 tablespoons butter
3 cups icing sugar
½ cup granulated sugar
¾ cup boiling water
3 to 4 tablespoons thin cream
½ chopped nuts

Melt the granulated sugar slowly in saucepan over low flame, stirring until light golden brown; add boiling water slowly stirring constantly.

Boil until it reaches consistency of thick syrup. Allow to cool.

Cream butter; add icing sugar gradually.

Add cold syrup and cream slowly until right consistency to spread.

To a third of this, add the chopped nuts, and spread between layers.

With the remaining plain icing, cover the top and sides of the cake.

Sea-breeze Frosting

2 cups sugar
2 egg whites
1 teaspoon golden syrup
1 cup approximately boiling water
1 teaspoon vanilla

Place in a saucepan over low heat the sugar, syrup and boiling water.

Stir until the mixture boils.

Then cook until it makes a thread, or when tested in cold water it forms a soft ball.

Remove from the fire and pour over the stiffly beaten egg whites.

Beat quickly until cold.

Add flavouring and continue beating until it is of the right consistency to spread.

Fillings

Delicious Chocolate Filling

This recipe is ideal for pies, tart shells or cream puffs. It will fill about 8 to 10 little pastries or tarts.

2/3 cup soft sugar
2 eggs or 2 egg yolks
1/3 cup sifted flour
1/8 teaspoon salt
1 bar sweet chocolate (7 ozs.)
2 cups scalded milk
1 teaspoon vanilla

Melt chocolate in double boiler, or over a pan of hot water, never over direct heat.

Also scald milk over hot water.

Mix the dry ingredients and the scalded milk very slowly, and beat with an egg beater until smooth.

Put back over the hot water in pan or double boiler and cook 15 minutes, stirring constantly until the mixture thickens, and afterwards occasionally (it will look like thick white paste).

Add eggs, slightly beaten, and beat with egg beater.

Cook in double boiler 3 to 5 minutes longer.

Remove from stove.

Add melted chocolate and beat with egg beater; add vanilla and cool. It will become very thick.

Fill small pastries with a tablespoon of this mixture, and a big dab of whipped cream on top.

Filling for Leftover Egg Yolks

½ cup sugar
4 egg yolks
½ cup cream
Lemon juice

Beat egg yolks until frothy.

Add the cream, sugar and enough lemon juice to make the right consistency.

Cook over hot water until it thickens.

Lemon Cheese Filling

This quantity will make a 2 lb. jar.

1/2 cup butter
2 cups sugar
6 egg yolks
4 egg whites
Grated rind of 2 lemons
Juice of 3 lemons

Put the ingredients into a pan and simmer gently until as thick as honey.

Synthetic Cream

This recipe is sufficient for a 2 layer cake.

1 cup castor sugar
¼ cup water
1 egg white
1 scant cup creamed butter
2 spoonfuls of rum, brandy or strong coffee for flavouring

Make a syrup with the sugar and water.

Boil for 5 to 6 minutes without stirring – must not crystallize.

Pour over the stiffly beaten egg white and whisk briskly for a moment.

Fold in creamed butter.

Flavour with the rum or brandy.

To make Mocha cream, substitute 2 tablespoons of cold, strong coffee for the rum.

Dear Reader,

We are very interested in your comments and feedback on this work. Please help us by commenting on this book. You can do so by leaving a review after reading it in your e-book reader or at the store of purchase. You can also e-mail us at the following address info@editorialimagen.com

For more books, visit the following site Editorialimagen to view new titles available and take advantage of the discounts and special prices we publish each week. You can contact us directly from there if you have any questions or suggestions. We look forward to hearing from you!

More Books

Desserts and Ice Creams - English Favourites: A selection of the best British recipes.

More than 130 desserts including boiled puddings, tarts, fruit tarts, desserts with gelatine, ice creams and much more!

Cakes - English Favourites: A Selection of the Best British Recipes

More than 70 cake recipes for every occasion, from a simple sponge cake to a wedding cake, including fruit cakes, gingerbread, shortbread, pastries, chocolate cakes, icings, fillings and more!

Spanish Related Books

Las Más Fáciles Recetas de Postres Caseros

Esta selección contiene recetas prácticas que, paso a paso, enseñan a preparar los postres, marcando el tiempo que se empleará, el coste económico, las raciones y los ingredientes.

Recetas Vegetarianas Fáciles y Baratas - Más de 100 recetas vegetarianas saludables y exquisitas

Si buscabas recetas de cocina vegetariana este libro de recetas veganas es para ti. El mismo es un recetario- que contiene una selección de recetas vegetarianas saludables y fáciles de preparar en poco tiempo. Este recetario incluye más de 100 recetas para toda ocasión, y contiene una serie de platos sin carnes ni pescados, con una variedad de recetas de Verduras, Huevos, Queso, Arroz, Ensaladas.

Recetario de Tortas con sabor inglés

Si buscabas recetas de cocina británica este libro es para ti. El mismo contiene una selección de recetas de tortas con sabor inglés. Este recetario incluye 80 recetas para toda ocasión, las cuales van desde lo más sencillo hasta lo más especial, como por ejemplo, una boda.

Recetas de Pescado y Salsas con sabor inglés

Recetas populares y a la vez muy fáciles, de la cocina británica. El recetario presenta diferentes maneras de cocinar el pescado, como así también tartas de pescado y salsas para acompañar el pescado.

Recetas de Sopas con sabor inglés

La sopa es un plato saturado de proteínas y nutrientes, es muy fácil de elaborar y además, apetece a cualquier hora del día. En la dieta inglesa la sopa es muy importante.